INTERN MANUAL

Inca Link Intern Manual

Copyright © 2014

ISBN: 978-1-935256-41-0

Ledge Press
PO Box 1652
Boone, NC 28607
www.ledgepress.com
ledgepress@gmail.com

INTERN MANUAL

Inca Link Values (MAC3)

M – Lifelong promoters of missions

A – Attitude is everything

C – Creativity is celebrated

C – Connecting people

C – Compassion. Service is a growth tool

My Commitment

1. GIVE 110%

2. CHALLENGE by choice

3. Be HERE now

4. CHOOSE JOY

5. LOVE covers it ALL!

TABLE OF CONTENTS

WELCOME NOTE

Hey Interns!

We have been praying for you and are excited about you coming to serve with Inca Link! This is going to be a great experience, and we thank God that you are a part of it. All of you have already met with Kayla Stevens and made it through the hoops of our application process, so congratulations! Now it's training time!

You guys need to know that in a real sense you will be seen as missionaries. You are representing Christ in another culture. It's a big responsibility. As career missionaries, Rich and I take it very seriously that you will be sharing our title. Although we want you to have a great time serving with Inca Link, you need to know right from the start that this is going to be hard work: physically, mentally, emotionally and spiritually. Remember that hardworking people have sacrificed their resources so that you can serve here. Don't let them down! Your safety is a priority to us, but it is also a priority that you truly get a sense of what is it like to be a missionary. This means you will be out of your comfort zone continually. Serving Christ in another culture is the best adventure around, but it isn't easy. You will need to empty yourself and depend on God COMPLETELY. It is a painful process, but it is the ultimate high and will change you forever! So that is what we pray for you. Are you ready?

This manual contains a basic "job description" for you, some guidelines for your day-to-day life as an intern, some facts that you need to know about the countries you are serving in, and the overall "big picture" vision of Inca Link. We don't ask a lot from you guys as far as training is concerned, so please read this manual and know it. If you know the information in it, you will be a better intern. When you are having a hard time being creative, your manual can give you ideas on debriefs and on working with teams. READ IT!

There are also some rules in here. We really have tried to keep the rules to a minimum, but from experience, realized we have to have some. All of them are guidelines to help you do your best and to be really focused as interns. There are two behaviors that will have you sent home immediately:

1. You intentionally hurt someone physically, sexually or emotionally.

2. You do not submit or respect your authorities.

You have experienced the challenge of raising support for this adventure, so you have already made it through one of the worst parts of being a missionary!

Thank you for doing this. Your raised money not only covers your food, housing, medical needs, and transportation, but also helps support long-term compassion and training ministries here in Latin America! Trust us to take care of you. Being a missionary will probably mean experiencing a different standard of living and require a good amount of sacrifice too. Please talk with us if making these sacrifices becomes a concern for you. If you have any support money remaining, or you are unable to complete your internship, those funds will be used to support Inca Link's greatest needs. it will go to our greatest needs in Inca Link. As a legal non-profit organization, we cannot return any of this money to you.

Despite the challenges, we know you are going to have a lot of fun! We LOVE our life! The truth is, no matter what you go through, attitude is the key. Because of our faith in Christ, we can have an attitude of complete peace. This attitude is contagious: it is contagious to the nationals you are serving, the other interns you work with, the missionaries you are helping, and the teams you lead! Keep it positive!

Thank you guys for being willing to serve, for getting out of your comfort zone, for raising money, for caring about the rest of the world and for coming to help us. We are excited, so BRING IT!

Rich and Elisa Brown

OVERVIEW OF INCA LINK

Inca Link International:
History, Mission, Vision, Strategy, Big Picture Chart

Inca Link On-Field:
Strategy, Ministries

INCA LINK INTERNATIONAL

Our History: Inca Link began when Rich and Elisa Brown, missionaries serving under the Christian and Missionary Alliance, saw the need to support compassion projects sponsored by national Alliance Churches. At the same time, there was an emergence of short-term teams wanting to get involved in missions. Together with their first intern, Lisa Merritt, they created Inca Link to meet these needs.

Our Mission: To reach the 300 million youth in Latin America with Christ's irresistible love.

Our Vision: Inca Link International exists to effectively resource and empower our Inca Link national organizations in their fulfillment of the Inca Link mission.

Our Strategy: To expose and connect youth and families to missions, ministry and the world; to build both national and international relationships that draw all parties closer to God; to partner with our national Inca Link organizations with holistic ministries that impact entire communities; to foster partnerships between teams and Inca Link projects that work toward being sustainable by the local communities.

The BIG Picture:

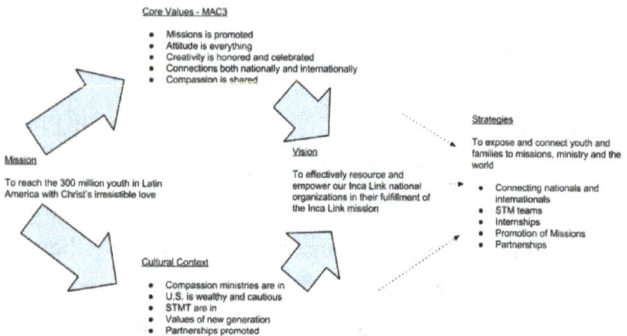

Core Values - MAC3
- Missions is promoted
- Attitude is everything
- Creativity is honored and celebrated
- Connections both nationally and internationally
- Compassion is shared

Mission

To reach the 300 million youth in Latin America with Christ's irresistible love

Vision

To effectively resource and empower our Inca Link national organizations in their fulfillment of the Inca Link mission

Cultural Context
- Compassion ministries are in
- U.S. is wealthy and cautious
- STMT are in
- Values of new generation
- Partnerships promoted

Strategies

To expose and connect youth and families to missions, ministry and the world
- Connecting nationals and internationals
- STM teams
- Internships
- Promotion of Missions
- Partnerships

YOU are a part of all that's happening in and through Inca Link.

INCA LINK ON-FIELD

Strategy: This is how Inca Link is reaching the 300 million youth in Latin America on the field:

1. Evangelism and Discipleship (Corban Ministries, Youth Encounter, outreach programs, supporting local church initiatives, sports ministries)

2. Training Leaders (Seminaries, Institutes, Youth Specialties, Camps)

3. Connecting People (Internships and Short-term teams: THIS IS YOU)

4. Compassion Ministries (Garbage dump, orphanages/children's homes, teen pregnancy center, prison ministry, etc.)

Ministries: There are key ministries we work with in Colombia, Ecuador and Peru to help us reach our goal. The following summaries give examples of how each country is implementing our strategy.

Inca Link Colombia

In Colombia we are concentrating on children and families struggling with physical, educational, social and spiritual poverty.

Oasis: Our sponsorship program enables children from the local community of Santa Cecilia to attend the children's program at the church five days a week. Children receive lunch, academic help, and most importantly receive daily Biblical teaching and a beautiful glimpse of Christ's love for them. Teams will have the opportunity to partner with the nationals in leading these programs.

Church Partnership: Interns will be involved in daily fellowship with the church of Santa Cecilia, helping with the services (small groups, worship, and prayer) and entering into the lives of the nationals.

Skills Training Workshops: Weekly workshops generate space to identify, develop and utilize the abilities and talents of youth and women. Many of whom are struggling with delinquency, these ministries offer precious time to form relationships and share the Gospel, while learning of their immeasurable worth as children of God.

Soup Kitchen: Holistic formation is the goal of these kitchens, aiming to meet the nutritional, academic, and social needs all routed through meeting the core, foundational spiritual need. Children come and receive their daily bread not only in the food provided but in homework help, mentoring, and discipling.

Youth And Adult Education: Alongside of professionals of diverse specializations, the Inca Link team offers a year long academic program for youth and adults in Bogota desiring to obtain their primary degree. This program also aids the students in finding stable employment.

Dicoco: Teaching single mothers and adolescent girls to sew and do handiwork. Many of them are struggling with delinquency, gangs, and/or drugs. This ministry opens space to form relationships, invite women to church and to share the Gospel.

Inca Link Ecuador

In Ecuador we are concentrating our compassion ministries on at-risk women and children.

Casa Blanca: Guest House where interns and teams stay when they are in Quito. Bed sheets, pillows, blankets, and fabulous food are all provided for you!

Casa Elizabeth: Our Teen Pregnancy Home exists to provide a safe transition into motherhood for teenage girls who find themselves with a crisis pregnancy. Teams can serve Casa Elizabeth by inviting the girls to minister alongside of the team in the other ministry areas. Also, teams may choose to bless the home with needed repairs or by helping to stock the closets with diapers, baby and maternity clothes and other supplies.

Ninawachi: A missions school located in the small farming town of Huaticocha, in the Amazon region of Ecuador. Its purpose is to provide education for surrounding indigenous communities who are interested in learning more about the Lord and His Word. Huaticocha is about 5 hours southeast of Quito.

Cumbre Alta: Sports-Discipleship program which exists to reach youth and children through sports. Teams can serve this program through sponsorships, connecting coaches from colleges in North America, participating in the sports camps, and leading a small group and even assistant coaching.

Tesoros: Orphan Ministry. At the time of this printing, Tesoros is focusing on a children's home in Manta. Teams can serve this program by assisting those who care for the children, helping in the kitchen, leading children's programs, as well as helping with the numerous maintenance and construction projects on the grounds.

Porto Viejo Garbage Dump: Partnering with the Porto Viejo Alliance Church youth group, every Saturday we go up and deliver water, some food supplies and gifts to the families living in the garbage dump and lead a program for children and their mothers.

In Peru we have concentrated on working with children, teenagers and families living in the marginalized neighborhoods surrounding the garbage dump.

Elim: Garbage dump ministry where we are taking resources to some of the most impoverished children in the world and sharing Christ with them. We are in the process of building church ministries in the garbage dump in Peru.

Mana: Our daycare center in Trujillo, for over 100 children whose parents work in the dump.

Pasitos de Fe: Inca Link is in the process of opening and staring to direct a children's home for at-risk kids in Trujillo, Peru, most of who are from the garbage dump area.

Inca Thakhi: Sandboarding is a growing sport in the deserts of Peru. This outdoor-discipleship ministry allows Inca Link Peru to reach the upcoming generation through outdoor activities, such as sand-boarding, mountain-boarding, skim-boarding surfing, and other team-building activities.

Church Cell Groups: It is so important to get involved in a small group in Trujillo. They need your encouragement and they are also inspired by your testimony to reach out to their community.

Amijai: Evangelism outreach to the community that surrounds the Children's Home. This ministry also provides ministries for the children and mothers of the neighborhood in which they learn of the love of Christ both in action and word.

MEET THE TEAM

Directors:
International, Colombia, Ecuador, Peru

DIRECTORS

RICH and ELISA BROWN and FAMILY // The Browns are the co-founders and president of Inca Link. They serve as regional missionaries with the Christian and Missionary Alliance and are based in Quito, Ecuador. They were youth pastors in Trujillo for 10 years, and have been in Ecuador since 2005. They have a passion for training youth leaders and have four awesome kids. The Browns are ultimately responsible for each and every intern who comes to serve with Inca Link. If there are problems with your internship, they will help solve them. Elisa is also the Communication Co-ordinator and touches base with each intern every Tuesday.

INTERNATIONAL

JOSEPH FISHER // Joseph was one of Inca Link's first interns and came to serve in Latin America for two consecutive summers. He now serves as our Chief Executive Officer and Chief Financial Officer. It is his job to build and manage effective administrative and financial systems. He and his wife Heather had their first child in 2013, beautiful baby Abby. They make their home in Wilkesboro, North Carolina.

KAYLA STEVENS // Kayla is the Intern and Team Coordinator. Based out of Minnesota, she serves to oversee the pre-field preparation of the Interns and Teams. She is passionate about what God is doing through these programs to glorify His name: as He delightfully uses them to support the ministries of Inca Link and to train the interns and teams in being His disciples. Kayla served as an Inca Link intern for 4 months in 2013.

COLOMBIA

BOGOTA

JHONNY ANDERSON // Jhonny is the Executive Director for Inca Link Colombia and has a passion for mobilizing young people to get involved in missions. He has a deep love for his country and hopes to share that passion with those who come to serve. Jhonny is also talented in music and ministers through that gift.

LUCY LANCHEROS // Lucy is married to Ricardo Rodriguez and has four grown kids. Her heart is to serve the least of these through social work projects in the impoverished sectors of Bogota. She is able to connect with kids in extremely challenging situations and works to prevent them from joining gangs. She serves as a leader with pastoral functions in the Alliance Church.

RICARDO RODRIGUEZ // Ricardo is the spouse of Lucy Lancheros. Ricardo is an expert in construction. He leads the construction of the majority of the projects and serves to meet the manual labor needs of the ministries. He also serves to help build the wells in the Amazon regions of Colombia.

LAURA RODRIGUEZ // Laura is a social worker who has committed fully to serve the ministries of Inca Link Colombia. She loves music and plays the drums. She is passionate in her work with children.

SAMUEL OTAVALO // Samuel is from Otavalo, Ecuador. and married to Mikaela. He studied language and is passionate about nature. He uses these passions and preparation as a tool to teach the children and youth about God's love in the different ministries.

DIANA ROJAS // Diana lives in the sector of Santa Cecilia, where she serves in the children's ministries. She is always with a contagious smile and joy. She is currently also a student.

KAREN YOPASA // Karen has helped with the validation process during this last year. She has a deep passion for serving this community and supporting the projects. She likes music and uses her talents during the Thursday youth programs.

QUITO

GUSTAVO CADENA // Executive Director of Inca Link Ecuador, Gustavo truly has a passion for training leaders and leading people in worship. After being a full-time youth pastor, he began his service with Inca Link in 2008. If you are living in Quito, Gustavo will be supervising your ministries and projects. He is also our expert on living, working and serving in Ecuador.

FABIAN and MABE TAMAYO //
Fabian and Mabe are using their gifts of hospitality to manage the guesthouse (Casa Blanca) for teams and interns. Passionate about cooking, they serve as the chefs. Fabian was a youth pastor and served in various churches. Mabe also serves Inca Link as a financial assistant.

NATE and KELLEY TAUBE //
Having grown up as missionary kids (Argentina and Ecuador respectively), Nate serves as the coach for Casa Deportiva Cumbre Alta and Kelley as the counselor for the Alliance Academy. Three years ago they packed up their 8-month old and traded the Chicago skyline for a view of the Andes mountains. Since then, they thought they'd ensure their biculturalism by adding another baby to the family: this one with an Ecuadorian passport! They moved here because they believe God will use them to help kids know His love.

PATRICK WATTS // Having been an intern with Inca Link for three years, Patrick finished up his engineering degree in plastics, worked in the field, and is now serving as a missionary for Inca Link. Originally from Pennsylvania, he has a burden for nationals and interns alike. Patrick is the Intern Coordinator in Ecuador and Colombia.

GIOVANNY and PAULINA GUZMAN-BRAVO // Giovanny and Paulina joined Inca Link in September of 2013 and serve as the primary caregivers to the young mothers and their babies in Casa Elizabeth. They also model a godly family to the young moms. They have two beautiful children, Lucas and Elizabeth.

MANDI HOWLETT // From Raleigh, North Carolina the Lord has given Mandi a child-like joy and the desire to show love to children and those in need. Mandi, having fallen in love with the culture, people, and the children, as an intern was led by the Lord to be Inca Link's Kindergarten teacher at the Alliance Academy International.

HUATICOCHA

MARK and CHERYL SHAFER // Mark and Cheryl have been missionaries in Ecuador since 2002, serving with Inca Link since 2008. After a short-term missions experience in the '90s, they made the decision to leave their business and follow the passion God had given them. They have worked with indigenous people in Ecuador, trained leaders in Nicaragua, and planted churches in both countries. They currently help host teams and interns at Huaticocha, as well as supervise the construction of Ninawachi Mission School. If you are in Huaticocha, Mark is your project supervisor. Mark and Cheryl will be your "heart monitors" checking in on your spiritual health and attitude as you live in a different culture.

JIM ZOSCHG // Jim is a two-time returning intern who, in 2012, took the step to work as a full-time missionary with Inca Link in Ecuador. Jim loves Latin America and its people. His passion is working in rural and indigenous communities, sharing the Gospel of Christ with those living without hope.

ALVARO VALLADERES // Originally from Nicaragua, Alvaro graduated from Cosecha Mundial Missions School and served as the Academic Sub-Director and professor at Somoto Missions School. In September of 2012, Alvaro joined Inca Link Ecuador and is planning the curriculum for Ninawachi Missions School in Huatichocha. He serves as a professor and administrator.

ULISES PINEDA // Ulises is from Somoto, Nicaragua, where he graduated from Cosecha Mundial Missions School. Ulises works in rural indigenous communities fulfilling the Great commission through evangelism and discipling new believers and strengthening small, struggling churches. He serves as a professor at Ninawachi Missions School in Huaticocha.

COAST

PERCY and GEMA FIGUEREDO
// Percy was a youth in Rich and Elisa's youth group in Trujillo, Peru. He is a founding member of Corban. While he was a missionary in Porto Viejo, he met Gema and they married in November 2012. They are ministering to youth in Porto Viejo, Ecuador and have a heart for missions. If you are serving in Porto Viejo, Percy will be your project supervisor.

WILL and AMANDA EASON
// Will and Amanda have been serving as youth pastors in Savannah, GA for several years. After a whirlwind introduction to Inca Link, and several interviews with Rich and Elisa, God called them (and their son, Emery) to serve as missionaries with Inca Link in the children's home in Manta. They packed their bags and obeyed God's call to Ecuador...SIGHT UNSEEN! "William" in Spanish is "Guillermo" (try saying that fast), but Will prefers his Spanish name to be Maximo! We like a bit of crazy in Inca Link. If you are serving in the children's home in Manta, Will and Amanda will be your project supervisors.

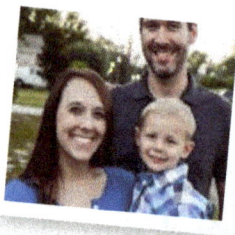

TRUJILLO

IGNACIO and MEYLIN MIRELES // Ignacio and Meylin are missionaries with Inca Link in Trujillo, Peru and have been serving faithfully in their role since May of 2012. Ignacio (born in Mexico and raised in Boise, Idaho) met Meylin (born and raised in Nicaragua) while he was leading a short-term mission team to Ecuador and she was serving as a full-time missionary with Mark and Cheryl Shafer. They fell in love and got married in 2010 and served full-time sharing the Gospel with indigenous communities in Ecuador until May 2012 when they were called to manage Pasitos de Fe in Trujillo, Peru. If you are in Peru, Ignacio and Meylin will be your "heart monitors," checking in on your spiritual health and attitude as you live in a different culture.

ELI VISALO CUEVA // Eli serves as Director of the Day Care Center (Mana) in Trujillo. He is able to connect with the children and their families in an incredible way. He enjoys his job thoroughly! If you are serving in Mana, Eli will be your project supervisor.

BRENT AND STEPHANY FREDERICK // Brent met Stephany on the World Race in 2011, which is the same year that Stephany started working at Inca Link. After the world race Brent returned to Trujillo, Peru to continue his relationship with Stephany, while they both did ministry at Elim, the garbage dump in El Milagro. During this time the Lord has continually laid a heavy burden on their hearts for the people living in this community. They got married on November 2014. In the future, they will continue to serve as a family in the ministry God has led them to.

JOSE CASTRO DIONICIO // Joca is a key member in Inca Link Peru. He heads up Inca Thakhi, our outdoor-adventure ministry, and has been called to start a camp for youth in Peru to share with them the Gospel and raise them as disciples. He is gifted in graphic-arts, passionate about seeing people come to Christ, and loves the Lord above all. He is a true servant and works alongside all the teams and interns in the work projects. If you are serving in Inca Thakhi, Joca will be your project supervisor.

VALENTIN // Valentin heads up our construction program at Pasitos de Fe. He has worked tirelessly on each of the buildings, and is always on hand for maintenance work. Although he knows very little English, he has been known to invent a whole new language to make sure things get done right! If you will be working in construction, Valentin will be your project supervisor.

BRENDA MOYA // Brenda Moya works with Inca Link Peru in ministering to the children from Amijai. Her hope is that this entire community will be brought to the knowledge of Jesus Christ and be transformed by Him. If you are serving in Amijai, Brenda will be your project supervisor.

DENICE MONICA RODRI-GUEZ // Denice was also one of the orignal youth in Rich and Elisa´s youth group in America Sur. She is a psychologist who works with our families at Mana. She is a hard worker who keeps us all organized at Pasitos de Fe. She helps Brent with logistics, picking people up, taking them to the doctor, or other

practical help that we might need. She is dedicated to helping the community as well as helping teams and interns.

YACKORRY MOYA // Yakcorry was invited to be volunteer with Inca Link Peru three years ago. With a passion to serve the Lord in the beautiful faith He has given her, she currently serves as a teacher in Mana discipling teenage girls. She also is in charge of housekeeping at Pasitos de Fe for the short-term teams.

CRISTINA TRUJILLO // Cristina was invited to serve the children of Victor Raul in the ministry of Amijai alongside of Brenda a year ago. The Lord uses the smiles on the children's faces and their desire to learn more about Him to set a passion in her heart to know Him deeper and fill her with His joy.

INTERNS

Expectations:
Attitude is Everything

Purpose

Our Goals for You

Support Structure

Internship Overview

Ministry & Creative Project

Team Leading

Summer v. Non-Summer

5 Personal Goals

Intern Contract

EXPECTATIONS

Our internship program is such that we expect a certain level of maturity from you. We expect our interns to be intentionally focused on the Christ, to discern God's guidance, to live responsibly in light of the fact that people have given sacrificially for them to serve overseas, and to be self-motivated and compassionate. Below is a grid of how your internship will be evaluated.

Attitude is Everything

Honestly evaluate yourself throughout your time on the field: How high is your level of service? How are your relationships within Inca Link, with the culture, and with others?

	Service	
	Low ⟶	High
High	Relational Time Waster Fun to be with Not dependable Don't get things done Sometimes motivated Signs of laziness Proactive in relationships	Relational Hard Worker Engaged Willing to serve in any way Flexible Shows fruit in ministry Lives above reproach Self-motivated Proactive MAC3-Lover Contract expert Good role model Has positive attitude
Relationships	Lazy Fearful Dependent Time waster Not dependable Self-involved Complainer Not flexible Bad reputation Poor role model	Hard worker Not flexible Not relational Know it all Not happy Working for work sake Self-motivated to work Proactive in service
Low		

SPIRITUAL PURPOSE

We believe that the Lord has sovereignly called you to this internship and we pray that, by the power of his Holy Spirit, He may grow you in greater depths of intimacy and satisfaction in Him alone. We pray that His name may be ever more glorified in and through you. May this internship serve to:

- deepen your commitment to Jesus Christ as related to discipleship and global Christians

- encourage the highest commitment to personal holiness through intentional focus on the Lord through daily spiritual-disciplines: consistent time in God's Word, journaling and personal prayer, fellowship, and communal prayer

- emphasize the call to unwavering commitment to team unity in the Body of Christ

- develop further a servant's attitude in humble and wise leadership

- strengthen the programs God has bestowed upon Inca Link

OUR GOALS FOR YOU

Our overarching goal is that God may grow your passion in His chief purpose of the glorifying of His name by all peoples and that He would direct you in seeing our call to share the glory of His grace in the Gospel that is for all peoples. In this our specific goals for you are:

- That you will be impacted in such a way that, even if you never return to Latin America, there will be life lessons that you take back to your home country. That these may impact your own local church and community for the growth of the Kingdom of Christ worldwide.

- That God will show you lifestyle changes that you can make to live a fully surrendered life for His Gospel mission.

- That you will become a life-long supporter and promoter of missions.

- That you will allow God to use you to impact the local churches and communities with your presence, testimony, relationships and service.

- That you will be an encouragement to the missionaries (North American and Latin missionaries) who are serving in different regions, recognizing them as brothers and sisters in the Body of Christ.

- That you will consider partnering with the Gospel work the Lord has bestowed upon Inca Link in the future (internships, promotion of projects, full-time mission service, donations, etc).

SUPPORT SYSTEM

We also understand that having a clear support system while you are overseas is important. We have a team set up to help you serve to your best capacity. Although our mission is to reach the 300 million youth of Latin America, we understand that you are part of that calling, and we want to see God work THROUGH you, as well as IN you. Your internship should not be a distraction to our mission, but a beautiful compliment. Never forget you are missionaries serving in the Body of Christ.

Here is the team you can count on while on the field:

1. **Rich and Elisa Brown** have setup the internship program and are responsible for your well-being and your training. You will meet them at the Amazing Race.

2. **Field Intern Coordinators:** Patrick Watts and/or Brent Frederick will coordinate your arrival and departures, any in-country traveling, your creative project, your daily routine, matching you with ministries, and making you feel at home.

3. **Heart Monitors:** We care about you and want to check on how you are doing during your time as an intern. Depending on where you are, either Mark and Cheryl, Gustavo, Elisa, or Ignacio and Meylin will make sure you are growing spiritually and thriving in your service.

4. **Project Supervisors:** No matter where you are serving, you will have direct supervisors helping your time of service be all that it can be for Christ. Although we do not want to be task oriented, we still believe it is important to have a project supervisor helping you give all you can.

5. **Communication Coordinator:** We are a big, international team and it can make you feel a little lost in the big picture. That is why every Tuesday we want you to connect with Elisa Brown—either through email, Skype, phone call, text or in person—to let her know how you are doing. It is just a short check-in. We like to hear a "high" of your week, a "low" of your week, something you accomplished that week, and what you need prayer for. Our entire team does this on Tuesdays, including missionaries, nationals, interns, and former interns. We call it Martes Marvilloso.

INTERNSHIP OVERVIEW

Your internship will consist of involvement in ministry sites and team leading. When you arrive on the field you will be able to visit all the sites. We fully trust the Lord to guide you in your specific ministry involvement.

MINISTRY

Internships provide a great opportunity to experience missions first hand. Being able to live in the culture, with the people, and ministering to those around you is an accurate representation of what missionaries do. We want your internship to be the best experience possible for you and glorifying to God in all that you do. You will be encouraged to develop a creative project that will last throughout the duration of your internship. This will give you the opportunity to use your gifts and passions to glorify God and advance the ministries during your time. We also want to help you have a sustainable impact on the Kingdom as you work with the team!

Creative Project

Purpose: Part of your involvement on the field is to fulfill a need or provide assistance in the community that is beneficial to the missionaries, ministries, and community, by using your gifts, skills, and interests.

Steps: (Steps 1-3 should be completed within the first two weeks of your internship)

1. Evaluate community/ministries to see where there is a need

2. Come up with a strategic plan/idea to fulfill this need

3. Check with missionaries/site coordinators for approval of idea

4. Do project throughout the summer

5. Set up a time to meet with site coordinators and discuss the progress of your project.

Some Ideas:

Soccer Camp: getting community together as an outreach

Art lessons: building relationships with a few people in the neighborhood, creating, and then displaying the artwork for all to see.

Child Sponsorship Program: develop a creative way to encourage both sponsors and children in communication.

Donations: find out what each ministry needs (material things) and communicate these needs to teams, or people back home and encourage them to donate.

Support: If a local church has a project in progress which needs financial support, help raise money for them.

Other: Cooking lessons, surfing lessons, English lessons, music lessons, video productions, prayer walks, babysitting, promotional material (i.e. calendar to sell back in the States) are additional ideas that you might be able to use.

Example #1

Mission: To engage the local churches in ministries Inca Link is currently involved in and in their local community through a short-term missions experience.

Vision: To expose local churches to the needs around them, in hopes of them becoming better missions supporters.

Goals:

- To organize a short-term missions trip within their own city

- Research the cost and logistics needed to make it happen

- Engage our local churches in Inca Link ministries

Timeline:

Step 1: Gather contacts that would be willing to help with this endeavor

Step 2: Set dates and cost for trip, talk with leaders at local churches

Step 3: Visit cell groups and do other types of promotion

Step 4: Final logistics

Step 5: Plan follow-up with each team member

Example #2

Mission: Our mission is to promote the value of education and potential of every child in Mana Day Care Center by providing the necessary resources and motivation through Christ-like love and community involvement. All steps will be taken to ensure that every child has the opportunity to reach their full potential through education.

Vision: Our vision is to see every child reach their potential through education and in doing so, break the generational cycle of poverty in the community.

Goals:

- Hold interviews with children and document the reasons why they are not attending school

- Find and plan practical ways for the students to attend school

- Track students' attendance and progress in school, by working alongside local schools

- Communicate with and receive support from parents, teachers and the community

- Hold monthly motivational sessions to discuss the value of education and build self-confidence

Create portfolios to highlight students' success in school and to document goals and struggles of each student in a positive way

Organize motivational field trips that promote education for a successful life

Set-up motivation charts

Show God's love through all aspects of the program

Timeline:

Week 1: Talk with the Director of the Day Care and get a list of all the kids not currently attending school

Week 2: Develop strategic questions to ask each child/family during the interviews. Set up interviews.

Week 3: Interview all the children who are not enrolled in school and develop a portfolio of each child

Week 4: Talk with a social worker and develop practical educational plans for each child

Week 5-6: Implement these plans with social worker and ILP staff. Register children for school, and buy school supplies and uniforms.

Week 7: Follow up with each child after they begin attending school

Week 8: Develop a motivational plan with the ILP staff to keep them in school and check up on their progress

TEAM LEADING

This position is a ministry of hosting and leading short-term mission teams. A team is usually around 15 people and the average time they are on the ground is 10 days. An intern will be with the team the entire time of the group's stay, and will be responsible for their overall care. These responsibilities include taking care of the physical, social, emotional, and spiritual needs of the team. The intern will be in charge of keeping open lines of communication with the nationals, the team leaders, and the team members. We encourage you to challenge the team, guide them, encourage them, and help them process what they are experiencing by debriefing each night. Many of the teams will be youth groups and we expect each intern to be a Godly example and encouragement to them. When taking the teams to different ministry sites and tourist attractions in the city, they will need to be well-informed of details that make the experience memorable for the team.

Being a Christ-like servant, to teams and nationals alike, is one of the most important qualities in this position. Some examples of this are: sacrificing comfort (bed, food, mosquito net, seat on the bus, etc), taking direction from nationals, displaying a positive attitude, being flexible, being prepared for the unexpected, or having a devotional/testimony ready to share at all times. This attitude of service also extends to how you interact with your co-intern. You will be working closely together, and will need to be united in decision-making and leading the team. Both interns will be responsible for helping each other in any way he or she can.

Your Role at Work Projects

1. The first responsibility is to help the team work!

2. Connect with the site host, introduce yourself and the team, and become acquainted

3. Cast the vision for the project; translate for your team any questions or comments to and from the nationals.

4. Find out what jobs there are and how many are needed for each job. Make sure there are enough tools for everyone.

5. Get them going! Start a group with the site host, then go and start the next group.

6. After starting all groups, go back and check in to see how they are doing or if they need anything. Let them know where you will be if they need translating or anything.

7. It is possible that you may not work on a job; you may be translating or getting materials the whole time. While walking around, encourage them, offer to get them water or to take a break.

8. It is good and healthy to sometimes take time NOT to work.

   - This cannot be everyday or every time there is work to do.

   - After you have helped everyone get started, tell them that you and your intern partner are going to take an hour together to prep, plan or work on finances. Go out of view from the work site. Come back to check on everyone before doing a job

9. Connect with your co-leader. Laugh together and pray together, or maybe take some time to just be.

10. There will also be times when you will need to work, when your team is tired out.

    • Inspire them with your actions: get in there and get dirty with them, and make your work fun! Lead by example.

SUMMER v. NON-SUMMER

We have always insisted that we want your internship to be a reflection of who you are and where your unique talents and abilities lie. We understand that if you are working in the areas that energize you most, we all gain from it. We spend a lot of time in our May training taking tests to help discover the things that energize you.

It is important that you know however, that a summer internship is very different from a non-summer internship. For those of you coming in the summer, you will be spending a large part of your time leading teams. This translates into a very structured routine, long days, more English speaking, being surrounded by North Americans, helping others digest what they see each day. It is a very important ministry that bears a lot of fruit.

For those of you coming during non-summer months, your intership will consist of reviewing our ministry projects and then deciding where we need the most help. You will need to be proactive and self motivated to give your all to these ministries. You will be on your own, getting around independently and working on your own. Your teammates will be primarily latinos, and you will be speaking a lot more spanish.

If you are coming as an Academic intern (one who receives college credit for their intership) your internship may look entirely different from those mentioned above. Your college will play a part in determining where you will need to invest your time, and your days will be determined by the types of projects you must be involved in to get credit and the amount of study hours you must put in.

No matter when you come, or if you receive official credit for your time here, we want you to realize you are an important part of the Inca Link team and we are thankful to God that you have come to serve here in Latin America.

We require each intern to come up with 5 personal goals to strive towards during their internship. Internships are designed with a lot of flexibility, so that you can be involved in specific things God calls you to. Whether this is improving in the language, connecting with nationals, or enhancing a ministry project, we want to help you achieve these goals. These goals may be altered during your internship. The Site Coordinators will meet with you periodically to talk with you concerning these goals, how you are doing on them, encourage you in them, and help you be successful in accomplishing these goals that you have set before yourself.

1.

2.

3.

4.

5

As an Inca Link intern, we ask you to agree to the following terms and "non-negotiables" listed below during your internship. Remember that we are working with the Christian and Missionary Alliance, and so we have to submit to their authorities and rules as well. Above all we are serving the Lord and desire to please Him first and foremost.

1. Have a saving knowledge and relationship with Jesus Christ

2. Be devoted to spending personal time with the Lord

3. Have an open heart for learning about and experiencing missions

4. Desire to build relationships

5. Promote missions

6. Have had at least one year of college

7. Meet with Browns (or missionaries) for personal discipleship, updates, and debriefs

8. Debrief every night, when with a team

9. Spending time in prayer with teams

10. Spending time with the least of these

11. Use your personality, gifts, and talents as you work and serve

12. Refrain from smoking, drugs, drinking, or relationships!

Inca Link Staff reserves the right to terminate any internship at any time for any reason.

I, _____, agree to abide by the terms listed in the Intern Manual. I also understand that all finances for my internship will stay with Inca Link if my internship is terminated early for any reason.

_____

Signature of Intern

_____

Date

MINISTRY SITES

Bogota, Colombia

Quito, Ecuador

Amazon Region of Ecuador

Coastal Ecuador

Trujillo, Peru

BOGOTA, COLOMBIA

Site Description

Your living quarters will be determined by the circumstances of your internship. You may be living with a host family from the church, a family of an Inca Link team member, or with other interns in Inca Link's guesthouse. You will serving in urban ministries in the capital city of Bogota and in rural ministries just outside of the city and accompanied by Inca Link team members.

Ministry Description

There are a variety of ministries in Bogota and surrounding areas including: mentoring and discipling children, youth and young adults through workshops, soup kitchens, soccer camps, building wells, leadership seminars, and academic programs.

What to Wear

Colombia experiences all four seasons in one day! Because of the elevation the weather can be warm during the day and then become quite cool during the evening. So our advice to you is to bring clothing that can be layered. Most people in the city dress like North Americans. At church, avoid wearing flip-flops or shorts; girls should only wear shorts while playing sports. Just remember, our goal is not to call attention to ourselves by the way we dress.

Food

You will have the opportunity to experience various types of food while you are here. You will be able to prepare your own food, share meals with families of the church and team members, or eat out at restaurants.

Contact Information

Carrera 5ta este N° 162 c 13
Bogota, Colombia

Jhonny Anderson
cell: +573138825200
email: Jhonnyandersonn@gmail.com

Lucy Rodriguez Lancheros
cell: +573012671241
email: encuentrocomed@gmail.com

Laura Rodriguez Lancheros
cell: +573185036539
email: laurarolats@gmail.com

QUITO, ECUADOR

Site Description

You will be living in Inca Link's guesthouse Quinta Casa Blanca while serving in urban ministries in the capital city of Quito. You are also expected to help out with logistics, cleaning, and preparations when teams come. Casa Blanca is located in a quiet neighborhood in the northern part of the city, with a breathtaking view of snow-capped mountains. You will receive an orientation for Casa Blanca upon your arrival. (Casa Blanca has wireless Internet access.)

Ministry Description

We have partnerships with numerous urban ministries in Quito including: orphanages, an after-school program for street-children, prison ministry, local church ministries, and a pregnant teen ministry.

What to Wear

It is said that Quito experiences all four seasons in one day! While it is located on the equator, the weather can also become quite cool because of the high elevation. So our advice to you is to bring clothing that can be layered. Most people in the city dress like North Americans. At church, avoid wearing flip-flops or shorts; girls should only wear shorts while playing sports. Just remember, our goal is not to call attention to ourselves by the way we dress.

Food

You will have the opportunity to experience various types of food while you are here. You will be able to prepare your own food, eat with teams Casa Blanca, or out at restaurants. During non-summer months you will often eat at the Brown's house on Tuesdays.

Contact Information

Fundacion Inca Link Ecuador
Calle D N74-285 y Calle Capri (N75)
Sector "Bellavista de Carretas"
Quito, Ecaudor

Rich and Elisa Brown
Rich's cell: +59399639812
Elisa's cell: +59399638988
Email: brown@incalink.org
skype: rebrown37

Gustavo Cadena
Cell: +59397938536 / +59396001452
Email: guscaf@gmail.com
Skype: guscaf1

AMAZON REGION OF ECUADOR
(Huaticocha and surrounding communities)

Site Description

The missionary team has a passion for reaching the indigenous people of Ecuador. Living among the people in Amazon communities, eating local foods, and traveling by river to remote communities in motorized canoes are just some of the exciting things to look forward to! (Huaticocha has very limited Internet access.)

Ministry Description

There are hundreds of communities with little or no Christian witness in jungle regions of Ecuador. The missionary team is passionate about reaching these communities. Inca Link has built a missionary training school called Ninawachi (which means "House of Fire" in Quichua) in Huaticocha, where the goal is to educate and prepare missionaries to go out and share the love of Christ with people in surrounding regions. They opened their doors in January of 2014. The student body is comprised mainly of indigenous youth, who will study and live on campus for two years. Part of students' training includes starting kids clubs and youth groups in neighboring communities. Ninawachi is one way the missionaries seek to fulfill their primary focus of evangelism and discipleship.

You will be helping at the Ninawachi Institute and working in the neighboring communities. We try to provide resources for classrooms, homes, and villages; if the community has a school, their resources are always very limited. Educating the people of these communities academically as well as on healthcare issues is a secondary focus.

Ministry Prep

Kids and youth programs must be prepared in advance, including crafts, songs, lessons, or dramas. The missionary team gives a great orientation and vision-casting for the school.

What to Wear

Come prepared with work clothes, including t-shirts and long pants. For safety reasons, NO shorts may be worn should any construction need to be done.. Bring modest bathing suits for swimming in the river and pants for church services. Bring a sweatshirt for cool evenings and protection against bug bites! Just remember, our goal is not to call attention to ourselves by the way we dress.

Food

While in Huaticocha, you will eat typical Ecuadorian fare. Local indigenous cooks will provide most of the food for when you are visiting communities, but we will eat sometimes in a restaurant. Tasting local cuisine is a great cross-cultural experience. Please at least pretend to like the food!

Contact Information

Mark and Cheryl Shafer
Cell: +593994783863
Email: shafer@incalink.org
Skype: charles.mark.shafer

Jim Zoschg
Cell: +593992336063 or +593995270522
Email: zoschg@incalink.org

Alvarlo Valladares
Cell: +593969913477
Email: avsoni777@yahoo.com

Ulises Pineda
Cell: +593991143369
Email: ulisespineda11@yahoo.com

COASTAL ECUADOR

Site Descriptions

Portoviejo is located on the coast of Ecuador, so it's nice and warm all the time. The people in Portoviejo are fun-loving and animated; they work hard and play hard, and you will have a great time doing the same thing! Expect to live with a family and learn a lot of

Spanish. Percy is the youth pastor at a new Alliance church plant; he and his wife Gema have a heart for missions and their enthusiasm is contagious. (Limited Internet access)

Manta on the other hand is not warm. The orphanage sits on a mountain in Manta and gets a cold ocean breeze, so you will need to bring a jacket or sweatshirt to wear even during the day. However, just five minutes down the mountain, you will be hot again! The children there are ready to be loved and the Easons are ready for some good help! (Limited Internet access)

Ministry Description

In Portoviejo, you will be working alongside the very energetic Alliance youth group. They have ministries in and around the city. They also minister to a few villages in that area that have struggling churches; youth there are encouraged to meet you and hear your story. Here you will get a good picture of what the established local church is doing to reach out to the communities around them. Visiting the elderly, working at the local orphanage, taking water and food to the garbage dump, planning and organizing youth group meetings will all be part of your ministry experience.

In Manta you will be helping with the many maintenance and construction needs. You will also be helping to feed the orphans, study with them, play with them, take them to appointments and church activities.

Ministry Prep

Get your testimony ready! Percy loves his youth to hear our interns' testimonies, so you will certainly have the opportunity to share. The youth group will help you get your testimony ready if you need it. If you have musical ability, it will be used. It is most important to prepare your heart for service and not shy away from the challenges presented to you.

In Manta, you will need to prepare your heart and eyes to see the needs around you. The orphans love attention, and it is good to love on them, but there are alot of physical needs that you might be tempted to ignore. Get ready to do the things you don't want to do, like cleaning, scrubbing, sanding, painting. It will all bring glory to God.

What to Wear

Follow the lead of the youth in Portoviejo as to what clothing is appropriate. Since it is a warm climate, shorts and tank tops are very common. However, dressing up for church is still customary. As it's cooler and slightly damp in Manta, come prepared with clothing that will keep you warm. Dressing in layers is advisable. Be prepared for cold nights here! Just remember, our goal is not to call attention to ourselves by the way we dress.

Food

The good news is that the coast of Ecuador is known for having the best food in the country! They are known to give large portions, so eat what you can, try everything offered to you, and share what you cannot finish. You will be eating in homes and out in restaurants.

Contact Information

Portoviejo:
Percy Figueredo
Cell: +593988706819
Email: percyfigueredo@gmail.com
Skype: percyfigueredo

Montañita Verde:
Will and Amanda Eason
Will Cell: +593987349343
Amanda Cell: +5930983921564
Email: eason@incalink.org

TRUJILLO, PERU

Site Location: About 9 hours north of Lima by bus

Site Description

Trujillo is located on the coast in northern Peru, with a population of about one million. Most of our ministries are located in the Victor Raul sector of Trujillo. It is a poor area, sandy and dusty. Inca Link asked the churches of Trujillo in 2006 what they thought was the greatest need in their community. Their response? "We need to get the children out of the garbage dump." So they determined to build a daycare center and children's home. In summer 2007, short-term mission teams helped fund and build the day care center (Mana), which now has over 100 children in attendance, while their parents work in the garbage dump. In 2008, we started building the Children's Home (Pasitos de Fe), and we hope to open the doors by middle of 2014.

Ministry Description

You will have the opportunity to take resources to some of the most impoverished children in the world and share Christ with them. There are church ministries in the garbage dump in Peru, a daycare for children of parents who work in the dump, a children's home for at-risk kids in Trujillo, and an outdoor ministry (Inca Thakhi) that seeks to reach the upcoming generation through outdoor activities, such as sandboarding, surfing, mountain boarding and other team building activities.

Ministry Prep

Kids and youth programs must be prepared in advance (i.e. crafts, songs, lessons, and dramas).

What to Wear

Shorts can be worn on the construction site, modest bathing suits for the beach, and pants for church services. No flip-flops outside of your home. Just remember, our goal is not to call attention to ourselves by the way we dress.

Food

Rice, potatoes, and chicken are commonly served foods. We have some great cooks out at the albergue, and you will also have the opportunity to buy groceries and make your own food. Occasionally we will eat in restaurants. When we are with a team, the churches often provide lunch. Peru has some of the best food in South America, so be ready to enjoy!

Contact Information

Trujillo:
Mz. N Lt. 22Miguel Grau, Sexta Fase Kunamoto-Los Libertadires
El Porvenir, Trujillo Perú

Ignacio and Meylin Mireles
Cell: +51941498890
Email: mireles@incalink.org

Brent Frederick
Cell: +51944260412
Email: frederick@incalink.org

TEAM LEADING

Philosophy of Short-Term Teams

Short-Term Team Overview

Pre-Field:
Team Prep Checklist

On-Field:
Info Chart, General Responsibilities (Connecting with Group Leaders, Debriefing, Church Service), Arrival Night, First Day, Final Day

Post-Field:
5 F's, Reciprocal Partnership v. Mutual Using

PHILOSOPHY OF SHORT-TERM TEAMS

Why do we do what we do? What is our main purpose for running short-term teams with Inca Link? How do we know if it is worth it? How do we know if we have done it well?

Generally short-term teams embark on their mission with the very best of intentions. They have heard the call of Christ to serve their neighbors or to make disciples and are excited to be obedient. The reality is that good intentions are just the beginning. If that is all a short-term team carries with them, then they will soon run into trouble. Unfortunately, it is quite possible for short-term teams to do more harm than good.

That is a very difficult concept for some. As harsh as it may sound, good intentions alone are not good enough. It is not good enough that you got on a plane to come down here. It matters very much what your attitude is as you come, and what it is that you are hoping to accomplish.

One note about terms, you may have noted that I am not saying 'Short-Term Mission Trips,' the most commonly used term. We intentionally choose not to use the word trip, as it inherently puts the focus on the one taking the trip. It makes it all about the ones who pack their suitcases and go somewhere, do something, and then return home.

The reality of STM is that it touches at least 5 different groups of people, and is certainly not simply about those with the suitcases. Know that for STM to be successful it should positively impact all five groups:

1. Those who leave their context (the ones with the suitcases)

2. Those who sent the team (the sending church and those who sent checks)

3. Those who are gracious enough to accept the team into their midst (ministry sites)

4. The entire community or context around those who accept the team (church, neighborhood, missionaries and community)

5. The missionaries (who should be blessed by your presence)

"God, praise Him, is already alive and well wherever it is that a STM team goes. Even if the destination is to non-believers, you can trust that God is already there and is already working. Your job is to merge into His traffic, participate in what He is doing, and then merge out of it, on to the next thing to which He has called you."

—Roger Peterson (from his book, Maximum Impact Short-Term Mission)

SHORT-TERM TEAM OVERVIEW

STM can generally be broken down into three distinct parts:

Pre-field

On-field

Post-field

We generally tend to dismiss parts one and three, and only focus on part two: time spent on-field. The reality is that as life-changing and impactful as the on-field part is, it is the least important of the three parts. I can hear some of you saying, "How do you figure that? On-field is the least important? But isn't that where we see God work, miracles happen, and lives changed?" We say this merely to highlight how important the other parts are, and how they too should bear life change.

The second most important part of STM is the time spent preparing to go on the field. The sad reality is that most people spend more time researching where they will go on vacation than where they will go on STM. They arrive at the host country, state, or site full of questions. Some of my personal favorites here in Ecuador have been questions as to where the polar bears and giraffes are!

The most important part of STM is the post-field t ime. Let's examine why. In 2006, North American Churches spent 1.6 Billion USD on mobilizing STM. Take a moment and try to imagine what could be done with $1.6 Billion. Are we getting $1.6 Billion worth of return out of STM? It can't just be about the 10 days that people are serving; it has to be about the REST OF THEIR LIVES! We want seeds to be sown here that will grow and spread in the lives of all 4 groups mentioned before.

Team Prep Checklist

The following checklist should be reviewed and completed before the team's arrival:

1. Instructions received for housing orientation.

2. Print the schedule for each intern and team leader.

3. Review the budget or other specific information/ arrangements regarding the team with your co-intern(s).

4. Make sure rooms are ready for arrival; know where they are and room # so that you are prepared to give instructions to the team upon arrival.

5. Cash for teams needs (and possible emergency) is in hand.

6. Confirm flight arrival time.

7. Make sure there is drinking water available and accessible.

8. Check-in and pray with co-intern prior to team arrival.

9. Clarify roles for the week. Who's giving brief orientation upon arrival, leading debriefs, etc

   - Meet team at airport in Inca Link Apparel, in order to be identifiable to the team

   - Connect with the Team Leader immediately after arrival.

   - Print off Guesthouse Manual

INFORMATION CHART

Organization	**Inca Link**		
Geographic Location	Colombia: Bogotá	Ecuador: Manta, Quito, Portoviejo, Huaticocha	Peru: Trujillo
Approximate Cost (Lodging & Food)	$900	$990	$970
Accommodations (Urban & Rural*)	Urban	Urban, Rural, and Extremely Rural	Urban
Type of Work	• Children/ Youth Ministry • Women's Ministry • Clean Water Initiative	• Orphanages • Mission School • Teen Pregnancy Home • Prison Ministry • Construction • Children's Ministry • Garbage Dump	• Dump Outreach • Outdoor Sports/Discipleship • Children's Ministry
Team Size	10 people or more (The largest group was 180 people.)		

Connecting with Team Leaders

1. Find them at the airport.

   - Immediately connect with them and show that you value them

   - Tell them who you are and learn a bit about them

2. Talk with them first thing in the morning or if possible, the night they arrive

   - Find a time when you can connect with them daily

   - Build a relationship with them: it will show that you value who and how they are

3. First day (not first night)

   - Find out what kind of ministry the team has planned (VBS, songs, skits)

   - Offer to preview it, to check out cultural faux-pas and to build confidence into what the students have planned

   - Find out if there are any special talents on the team or Spanish speakers

- Find out what donations they've brought and establish when or where it is appropriate to give it away

4. Talk about each debrief time before it happens with the team leader

   - Establish who will do what, how you will work together

   - We are there to support

5. Bottom Line – The intern's job is to SUPPORT the team leader.

   - Your job is to help him/her to lead the best way that they can.

   - There will be a time to step up and a time to step down.

   - Remember, the team leader will be returning to the states with their team, and the team interns will not.

Debriefing

What is debriefing? Group sharing/reporting/processing.

Why do we do it? To help team members process what they have been seeing and experiencing. To help them discover why God has brought them on this Short-Term Mission Experience. What does God want to change in them when they get home! How can they be life long promoters of Missions?

When do we do it? EVERY night after dinner, or before going to bed.

How do we do it?

- Meet with the team leader 15 minutes prior to debrief and discuss with them what you would like to talk about. Check to see if they have any ideas or anything they want to talk about.

- The following should be considered.

- time/place/environment/ground rules

- listen, don't judge

- expect the irrational (don't be shocked or surprised)

- affirm vulnerability/honesty

- don't be afraid of tension…unresolved stuff

- help and encourage people to express themselves

- nobody is forced to talk

Questions to Ask

1. What can I learn about the people of God, about the church, about community?

2. What can I learn about how culture impacts the way we live and understand the Gospel?

3. What can I learn about justice, economics, poverty, and politics?

4. What can I learn about what it means to be a follower of Christ?

5. What can I learn about a globally appropriate lifestyle (stewardship)?

6. What can I learn about my calling in life, work, and ministry?

7. One word to describe your day and why.

8. Give your high and low for the day, and your hope for tomorrow.

9. What needs to change in my attitude, in my life, in my future?

Some ideas for debrief depending on activities of the day.

1. First days: What is your first impression of the city and the culture here? Let's start thinking about why God has brought you to this city and on this missions experience. What is He trying to teach you through this time? What does he want to change in you back home?

2. After experiencing church: What are the differences between Latin churches and our churches back in North America? What did you notice?

3. First construction days: What are your impressions about working construction at the work project? What were some of the things you needed to do to lessen your frustrations?

4. After doing a children's program: How did you feel about the children's program? How are the children different or the same to our kids at home? What can we do differently tomorrow?

5. Half way point: How is everyone feeling now that we are half way through the experience? What has God been teaching/telling you so far? Do the encouragement beads or something similar that will encourage the team and bond them.

6. After visiting the garbage dump, Seniors Home, orphanage, etc: What did you think of the _____?

What impacted you the most there? How has seeing what you did, or experiencing what you did, going to help you make a change in the future, or a difference in these type of ministries back home?

7. When you can't think of anything: A high and a low of the day are always thought provoking. You can also have each one describe the day with one word, and then explain why they chose that word.

8. A tourism day: What did you think of the tourism? How was the time on the mountain? Are you listening to God and what He has for you? How can be preparing to go home? Start talking about the Five F's. Do Beads!

9. Final day: Final Debrief! What has God been telling you through this time? What will change when you go home? How will you become an ambassador for missions?

Church Services

1. Prepare your team before entering.

2. Challenge them to look around and see differences and similarities from their home church services.

3. Challenge them to use the service as a time to pray, for the team, for the nationals that they see in the service, for themselves.

4. As an intern, pay attention to the service, and afterwards give an overview of what the sermon was about.

5. Be a bridge for them, across the cultural gap.

6. If given the opportunity, introduce your team and team leaders. Explain who they are and why they are here.

7. Be ready to translate.

8. Debrief the experience, talk about what they saw and felt.

ARRIVAL NIGHT ORIENTATION

This is an important night for you and the team. This is where you establish who you are: that you are there to help them through the week and that you are available for them. You will be with the team each day they are on the ground. You are also there to support the missionaries.

1. Welcome: We're glad you are here!

2. Schedule: Tonight, tomorrow, and how to prepare for the day

3. Living Rules and Helpful Tips: Please refer to Guesthouse Manual

4. Important Reminders:

- Toilet Paper: place it in the trashcan next to the toilet.

- Water: Do NOT drink tap water. Use the water provided. Refill at the guesthouse or, when out, buy bottled water. Everyone should have a water bottle with their name on it. Remind the team to drink lots of water! Brushing your teeth in the tap water is fine.

- Altitude: If you are in Quito, discuss altitude sickness, how to prevent and minimize it.

- Please respect the property in general. Do not take blankets/pillows on the bus or off the property.

- Remember to always turn off the lights when leaving a room.

- Hot water comes on automatically; wait about two minutes for it to heat up. Encourage the team to be courteous and eco-friendly, and take a 4-minute shower. Teach by example.

- There is Internet access for interns and team leaders only. We really encourage team leaders to collect phones from team members, so that they can truly unplug. If the team leader is in disagreement, WE DON'T COLLECT phones, but we continue to encourage the team to unplug. This means you as interns should try to be a good example and use the internet only when absolutely necessary, and not in front of team members.

- Safety issues: Stay put tonight. Do not go out for a late night snack. We will review safety guidelines more in the morning.

5. Importance of Attitude: What you give is what you get. If you give 5%, you will receive 5% in return. If you give 110% you will get that much more in return.

6. Availability: Make sure the team knows you are available to answer questions. Hang around with them if they are staying up. Get to know them.

FIRST DAY ORIENTATION

Start by introducing yourself and give a brief biography…testimony…or job description.

It is a good idea to start orientation by asking groups what they know about Ecuador, Peru, or Colombia.

If you are working in pairs, try to share this orientation.

1. Give overall picture of the country they are working in. (See Quick Facts).

   Country, Climate, Culture, Currency

2. Give Cultural Overview

   Greetings/Goodbyes

   Acceptable dress and behavior

   American stereotypes

3. Give Picture of Alliance Ministries in Latin America

   Beginnings

   History

   Needs

4. Culture Shock: It is normal! We all go through it. We all deal with it in different ways. If you are "freaking out" let us know. We will not ask you to do something that you absolutely refuse to do; we will look after your safety, but we do want you to get out of your comfort zone.

5. Language: It may be frustrating just to talk. Learn to laugh a lot, even at yourself and enjoy learning.

It's all about learning! Ask who knows Spanish? You also communicate through body/eyes/love.

6. Schedule: It is important to go over the schedule for their trip in general

7. Sickness: Tell them it's important for them to communicate about sickness with intern leaders

8. Safety: Use a buddy system at all times

9. Inca Link Contract

10. Rich's Infamous Wisdom Time: Tell the Chinese Fable

11. Lay Foundation of Christ-Centeredness: Start guiding them through this experience by asking them "why has God brought you on this experience and what does He want to teach you? What stones will you pick up along the way? Let's start keeping our hearts open to what God has for us."

12. Take questions from the group!

FINAL DAY

Final Debrief

1. Worship

2. Remind them of all they have done.

3. Share the 5 F's

4. Review the 3 parts of a missions experience (pre-field, on-field, post-field)

5. Say one practical thing they will change when they go home.

6. Share scripture with them, ask questions, allow sharing, and encourage honesty.

7. Pray for the team as they return to make a big impact in the 4 different areas.

8. Thank them and remind them of eternal impact.

9. Give out bracelets, shirts, brochures, prayer cards, etc.

10. Evaluations

Checklist

The following tasks need to be completed the day of/ day following the departure of your team.

1. Turn in all receipts to whoever is in charge of them.

2. If any donations need to be delivered to specific ministries, do that.

3. General donations should be organized and set aside for Inca Link Ministries

4. Reconcile finances and prepare report...turn it in!

5. Write a personal thank you email to the team leader and team.

6. Submit contact information of each team member to incalink@gmail.com

7. Review evaluations and turn them in to Site Coordinators.

8. Complete the Short-Term Host Debrief Form (each host)

9. Check-in with Intern partner. Anything else that needs to be discussed, prayed about, resolved, handle it ASAP.

10. Meet with site coordinators, or your supervisor to debrief your team.

5 POSSIBLE STAGES OF REENTRY (5 F'S)

The following list is the cycle you may go through emotionally, and the stages of adjustment as you re-enter home.

Have Fun (honeymoon)

Flee (avoidance)

Fight (anger, criticism)

Fit In (tolerance of differences)

Be Fruitful (creative engagement)

Fun

"I can't wait for a hot shower"

"I really missed you"

"I never thought a hamburger would taste so good"

You're glad to be home. It's great looking at pictures of your trip. You feel changed in your life, your relationship with God, and your vision of the world. You're ready to do things differently.

Flee

"Everyone here is so busy. Life seems so fast"

"I hate the freeways"

"No one seems to be interested in my experience. They only ask me, "How was your trip?""

You're discouraged by how materialistic, impersonal and busy life seems to be. You feel alone and miss the community you experienced with your team. People seem to be preoccupied with petty concerns, and easily depressed by silly issues-compared to the faith in God, joy and community you witnessed on your trip. You wish you could return. Somehow life felt more real, more solid, more significant there than it does here. Because you can't, you find yourself spending lots of time reliving memories, looking at pictures, trying to make contact with your team members. However, even that is hard because you (and they) are being swept up in the pressure and busyness of life here.

Fight

"People seem to take their faith so much more seriously over there"

"My church service seems so passionless"

"People are more interested in expanding their saving account than in saving the lost"

You find yourself actually feeling depressed about life here. People seem indifferent to the real issues in life. Even the church seems to foster a self-indulgent, self-preoccupied spirituality. Money dominates everything. You're becoming highly critical of life in the US, and speak out against what you see. When you're silent, you find yourself feeling spiritually superior, as if you understand better than others.

Fit In

"I can't live here like people do there. I tried to live differently but it's impossible"

"The cost of living is so much higher here. I have to accept it"

"I'm losing all my friends because they view me as a "mission fanatic"

The pressure to fit in: Now you find yourself simply seeking to fit in. The press of responsibilities has taken hold and it's simply too hard to keep focused on your experience over there. The memories are beginning to fade and you haven't been able to find ways to live differently in light of what you've experienced. You promised you would write the people you were with, but have barely had time to send a postcard.

The longing for another short-term mission trip: You find yourself longing for another short-term mission trip. Maybe that will help you recapture the feeling of your life counting for the Kingdom that you experienced before. That might stimulate your spiritual growth and draw you back into a sense of community.

An aborted process: Unfortunately, many people stop here. This ends their re-entry process. Their trip remains a distant memory.

Fruit

It should be your goal from the moment you begin the process of preparing for STM to work toward this stage in the re-entry process. How is your life going to be different for having gone on STM? What is God working on in you through this experience that will change how you live for the kingdom afterward. This is where the vocabulary can change from 'spending/wasting' money through STM, to 'investing/multiplying resources' through STM.

(Adapted from Lisa Espineli Chinn, "Reentry Guide for Short Term Mission Leaders," Orlando: DeeperRoots Publications p. 14, used by permission of the author)

RECIPROCAL PARTNERSHIP v. MUTUAL USING

The second half of how we define success in Inca Link for STM revolves around the idea of reciprocal partnership instead of mutual using. Lets find new ways to help each other.

We are giving a Prayer Card and a Faith Promise card to everyone so that they can be involved in the long run of missions. We want each person to commit to pray and give on a monthly basis for missions. We need your prayers as your missionaries. We encourage giving to happen through the Great Commission Fund in the U.S, or to the Global Advance Fund in Canada.

We then, commit to supporting you and your groups on these short-term (converted into a long-term) missions experiences. Our goal is for you and us to promote missions better every day.

(The above information includes resources taken from the National Consortium for Short- Term Mission, Roger Peterson, Dr. Tim Dearborn, and Rev. Roberto Guerrero, as well as life experiences in both leading and hosting short-term teams.)

WHEN HELPING HURTS
(Steve Corbett and Brian Fikkert)

We recommend this book to every missionary and intern we meet. It is the best book on the subject of how to help others struggling in various kinds of poverty without harming them. Please read the book and look over the following excerpts.

In your own words define "poverty."

_____

_____

_____

_____

Excerpt from pages 52-53

Below is a small sample of the words that the poor have used to describe their own situation:

For a poor person everything is terrible—illness, humiliation, shame. We are cripples; we are afraid of everything; we depend on everyone. No one needs us. We are like garbage that everyone wants to get rid of. –Moldova

When I don't have any [food to bring my family], I borrow, mainly from neighbors and friends. I feel ashamed standing before my children when I have nothing to help feed the family. I'm not well when I'm unemployed. It's terrible. –Guinea-Bissau

When one is poor, she has no say in public, she feel inferior. She has no food, so there is famine in her house; no clothing, and no progress in her family. –Uganda

The poor have a feeling of powerlessness and an inability to make themselves heard. –Cameroon

If you are hungry, you will always be hungry; if you are poor, you will always be poor. –Vietnam

While poor people mention having a lack of material things, they tend to describe their condition in far more psychological and social terms than North American audiences. Poor people typically speak in terms of shame, inferiority, powerlessness, humiliation, fear, hopelessness, depression, social isolation, and voicelessness. North American audiences tend to emphasize a lack of material things such as food, money, clean water, medicine, housing, etc.

Page 55

If we believe the primary cause of Poverty is...	Then we will Primarily Try to...
A Lack of Knowledge	Educate the Poor
Oppression by Powerful People	Work for Social Justice
The Personal Sins of the Poor	Evangelize and Disciple the Poor
A Lack of Material Resources	Give Material Resources

Page 57-58 – see figure 2.1

The Biblical Framework of Relationships

Relationship with God

Relationship with Self

Relationship with Others

Relationship with the Rest of Creation

These relationships are the building blocks for all of life. When they are functioning properly, humans experience the fullness of life that God intended because we are being what God created us to be. In particular for our purposes, when these relationships are functioning properly, people are able to fulfill their callings of glorifying God by working and supporting themselves and their families with the fruit of that work.

Page 62

"Poverty is the result of relationships that do not work, are not just, that are not for life, that are not harmonious or enjoyable. Poverty is the absence of shalom in all its meanings."

– Meyers' description of the fundamental nature of poverty

Page 78

Poverty Alleviation is the ministry of reconciliation: moving people closer to glorifying God by living in right relationship with God, with self, with others, and with the rest of creation.

Material Poverty Alleviation is working to reconcile the four foundational relationships so that people can fulfill their callings of glorifying God by working and supporting themselves and their families with the fruit of that work.

A helpful first step in thinking about working with the poor in any context is to discern whether the situation calls for relief, rehabilitation, or development. In fact, the failure to distinguish among these situations is one of the most common reasons poverty-alleviation efforts often do harm.

"Relief" can be defined as urgent and temporary provision of emergency aid to reduce immediate suffering from a natural or man-made crisis (i.e. "Stop the bleeding"). The key feature of relief is a provider-receiver dynamic in which the provider gives assistance—often material—to the receiver, who is largely incapable of helping himself at that time.

"Rehabilitation" begins as soon as the bleeding stops: it seeks to restore people and their communities to the positive elements of their pre-crisis conditions. The key feature of rehabilitation is a dynamic of working with the tsunami victims as they participate in their own recovery, moving from point 2 to point 3.

"Development" is a process of ongoing change that moves all the people involved-both the "helpers" and the "helped"—closer to being in right relationship with God, self, others, and the rest of creation. Development is not done to people or for people, but with people. The key dynamic in development is promoting an empowering process in which all the people involved—both the "helpers" and the "helped"—become more of who God created them to be, moving beyond point 3 to levels of reconciliation that they have no experienced before.

By far one of the biggest mistakes that North American churches make is in applying relief in situations in which rehabilitation or development is the appropriate intervention."

Page 115

Avoid Paternalism

Do not do things for people that they can do for themselves.

Resource Paternalism

Spiritual Paternalism

Knowledge Paternalism

Labor Paternalism

Managerial Paternalism

Chapter 7: "Doing Short-Term Missions Without Doing Long-Term Harm"

Please carefully read this chapter!

Page 161

"There were 120,000 in 1989, 450,000 in 1998, 1,000,000 in 2003, and 2,200,000 in 2006. The numbers reflect a tsunami of epic proportions, a tidal wave of American short-term "missionaries" flooding the world. The cost? Americans spent $1,600,000,000 on Short-Term Missions (STM) in 2006 alone."

Read the Elephant and Mouse Story

Page 171

If you (or your church) received a phone call from a friend in Switzerland asking you to: "You can choose between our sending thirteen people this summer to help with your VBS or our giving you the $25,000 it will cost to send the team," what would you choose? Why?

_____

_____

_____

_____

CULTURAL SENSITIVITY

Crossing Cultures

Quick Tips for Living in Latin America

Culture Entry Model

CROSSING CULTURES

As you cross into the Latin culture, with its many subcultures, strive to keep an open mind. Remember, just because something is different doesn't mean it is wrong. Ask God to help you see the Colombian/Ecuadorian/Peruvian people as He sees them. Try to understand why things are done differently than the way you would do them. Learn to appreciate the differences.

Remember you are the visitor; you have the different opinions and odd perspectives. You are a guest who has been given the privilege of visiting this country by the local government.

1. Do not judge the value system you will encounter according to your own cultural norms.

2. Remember that the missionaries you will be meeting have dedicated themselves to ministering to and with the people of Latin America. They will be happy to discuss the country and culture with you. However, when speaking with them, avoid criticizing the country or its people.

3. Control your temper! Facial expressions and body language speak louder than words.

4. Many Latin Americans speak or at least understand English, so only say what you want understood.

5. Most Latin Americans are very patient and forgiving of bad Spanish. Use all of the Spanish you can; "por favor" (please) and "gracias" (thank you) are very much appreciated.

6. Avoid discussing politics with your new Latin friends.

7. Be prepared to shake hands with/kiss everyone you meet. You will also shake hands/kiss when you say goodbye, even if you have only exchanged a few words.

8. Share your faith when you have the opportunity.

9. Be prepared, you will see nursing mothers in public! Don't stare!

10. You will encounter many beggars. A coin is an acceptable gift if you choose to give one, but it is not necessary. View these people as Christ views them!

11. If you are from North America, introduce yourself as a "North American." We are Americans too: "South Americans!"

12. When giving your testimony, be culturally sensitive. Many of the people to whom you will be speaking are much poorer than you and will have a different set of values.

13. Most importantly: If you are unsure of what to do in a situation, step back and let the missionaries take the lead. You will learn a lot by observing.

QUICK TIPS for LIVING IN LATIN AMERICA

1. Be flexible! The best-laid plans are often changed by outside influences. Be prepared to go with plan "B" or even plan "Z."

2. Be aware! Do not leave anything of value unattended. Cameras, tools, and electronics tend to grow legs and wander off in South America. Pickpockets are active in crowds.

3. Be discreet with your money. Your spending money could be a month's wages for someone.

4. Avoid food cooked by street venders.

5. The rule for fruits and vegetables is: If you can peel it, you can eat it! Otherwise, it needs to be cleaned. Instructions will be given for washing your own fruits and vegetables.

6. Scrapes, cuts and rashes should receive immediate attention. Your body has not built up immunity to tropical bacteria.

7. Wash your hands often and keep your hands out of your mouth.

8. For safety and protection from loss or damage, leave jewelry at home. A good rule of thumb: if you would care if it were stolen/lost, don't bring it!

9. Drink only purified/bottled water.

10. If you are in Ecuador, because of the change in altitude and climate, you will need to drink plenty of liquids. Purified water is best. Soft drinks and coffee can increase dehydration!

11. Toilet facilities may be scarce and toilet paper is rarely provided. Plan ahead. If a wastebasket is beside the toilet, it is usually an indication that

the T.P. is not to be flushed. This is the case in most homes, businesses, and public places.

12. When exploring away from the main group, stay in groups of 3 or 4. Girls should always be accompanied by at least one guy.

13. Remember, for all practical purposes, pedestrians do NOT have the right of way! Be alert when crossing streets and roadways.

14. When riding the public buses or trolley, please be considerate of women with children and the elderly. Offer them your seat.

15. Diarrhea is part of international travel. In Ecuador, the change of altitude, food and travel all contribute to this. Be prepared! In Peru, we can't blame it on the altitude, but we still get sick.

Attitude is Everything: We need you to have the best attitude possible. Give up your seat to the team members and go the extra mile. Serve others with all of your heart; don't make others serve you. Attitude is everything. Show that yours is fantastic and positive because it is contagious!

QUICK FACTS

Colombia

Ecuador

Peru

COLOMBIA

FULL COUNTRY NAME: Republic of Colombia

AREA: 1,138,910 sq km

POPULATION: 45,745,783; Bogotá (capital): 7,674,366 (Literacy: 93.6% Life Expectancy: 75.02 years)

PEOPLE: 58% Mestizo, 20% White, 17% Multi-Racial, 4%, Black, 1% Amerindian

LANGUAGE: Spanish (official language)

RELIGION: 90% Roman Catholic, 10% Other

GOVERNMENT: Republic (Executive Branch dominates government structure)

PRESIDENT: Juan Manuel Santos Calderon

CURRENCY: Peso (1942.22 per USD)

GDP: $366 billion USD ($11,000 per capita)

EXPORTS: petroleum, coal, emeralds, coffee, nickel, cut flowers, bananas, apparel AGRICULTURAL PRODUCTS: coffee, cut flowers, bananas, rice, tobacco, corn, sugarcane, cocoa beans, oilseed, vegetables; shrimp; forest products

INDUSTRIES: textiles, food processing, oil, clothing and footwear, beverages, chemicals, cement; gold, coal, emeralds

LOCAL TIME: Eastern Standard Time Zone (same as NYC) from November-March; Central Standard Time from April- October. Colombia no longer observes Daylight Savings Time.

CLIMATE: tropical along coast and eastern plains; cooler in highlands

TERRAIN: flat coastal lowlands, central highlands, high Andes Mountains, eastern lowland plains (Llanos)

ELEVATION EXTREMES:

Lowest Point: 0 m (Pacific Ocean)

Highest Point: 5,775 m (twin peaks Pico Cristobal Colon and Pico Simon Bolivar)

FULL COUNTRY NAME: Republic of Ecuador

AREA: 109,483 sq. miles (about the size of the state of Colorado)

POPULATION: 15,439,429; Quito (capital): 1.6 million (Literacy: 91.6%, Life Expectancy: 76.15 years.)

PEOPLE: 72% Mestizo, 15 % Indigenous, 7% Afro-Ecuadorian, 6% White

LANGUAGE: The official language is Spanish. In addition, 22 indigenous languages, including Quíchua, are spoken throughout Ecuador. In Quito, English is spoken by a large number of people, including North Americans, expatriates and some Ecuadorians.

RELIGION: 95% Roman Catholic, 3.4% Evangelical. Freedom of religion is enjoyed.

GOVERNMENT: Democracy-Presidential Republic

PRESIDENT: Rafael Correa

CURRENCY: US Dollar (as of 2000, when the Sucre was eliminated). Ecuadorian coins have been minted in values equal to American coins and are concurrently in circulation.

GDP: 84.53 billion USD (GDP per capita: $5,456.43)

EXPORTS: Petroleum, bananas, cut flowers, shrimp, and cacao.

AGRICULTURAL PRODUCTS: bananas, coffee, cocoa, rice, potatoes, manioc, plantains, sugarcane; cattle, sheep, pigs, beef, pork, dairy products; fish, shrimp; balsa wood

INDUSTRIES: petroleum, food processing, textiles, wood products, chemicals

LOCAL TIME: Eastern Standard Time Zone (same as NYC) from November-March; Central Standard Time from April- October. Ecuador does not observe daylight savings time.

CLIMATE: Ecuador, with its four distinct geographical regions, has a varied climate as well.

The Sierra, where Quito is located, is mild throughout the year due to the high altitude (9,350 ft). Temperatures range from 55-78° F year round, with an average of 64°. Quito is referred to as "the city of eternal spring," where a typical day can be sunny in the morning, cool and cloudy in the early afternoon, rainy in the late afternoon, and cool and clear in the evening. Typically, the rainy season occurs from October to May.

The Costa (the coast) is warm and humid during the entire year (76-90° F, with an average of 83°). Rainy season is usually from December until May.

The Oriente (the jungle region) is warm and humid. The rainy season is from December to February. August through October are the driest months.

The Galapagos Islands enjoy warm and dry weather year round, with an average yearly temperature of 85° F!

PERU

FULL COUNTRY NAME: Republic of Peru

AREA: 1,285,216 sq km (slightly smaller than Alaska)

POPULATION: 29,849,303; Lima (capital): 8.769 million (Literacy: 89.6%, Life Expectancy: 73 years)

PEOPLE: 45% Amerindian, 37% Mestizo, White 15%, 3% Other

LANGUAGE: Spanish (official language)

RELIGION: 81.3% Roman Catholic, 12.5% Evangelical, 6.2% Other

GOVERNMENT: Constitutional Republic

PRESIDENT: Ollanta Humala

CURRENCY: nuevo sol (PEN) per US dollar: 2.81

GDP: 197.1 billion USD ($6,573.04)

EXPORTS: copper, gold, zinc, tin, iron ore, crude petroleum and petroleum products, natural gas; coffee, potatoes, asparagus and other vegetables, fruit, apparel and textiles, fishmeal

AGRICULTURAL PRODUCTS: asparagus, coffee, cocoa, cotton, sugarcane, rice, potatoes, corn, plantains, grapes, oranges, pineapples, guavas, bananas, apples, lemons, pears, coca, tomatoes, mango, barley, medicinal plants, palm oil, marigold, onion, wheat, dry beans; poultry, beef, dairy products; fish; guinea pigs

INDUSTRIES: mining and refining of minerals; steel, metal fabrication; petroleum extraction and refining, natural gas and natural gas liquefaction; fishing and fish processing, cement, textiles, clothing, food processing

LOCAL TIME: Eastern Standard Time Zone (same as NYC) from November-March; Central Standard Time from April- October. Peru does not observe Daylight Savings Time.

CLIMATE: Varies from tropical in the east to desert in west; temperate to frigid in the Andes. Trujillo (where Inca Link's ministry site is located) is known as the City of Eternal Spring and has mild temperatures year-round.

TERRAIN: Western coastal plain (costa), high and rugged Andes in center (sierra), and eastern lowland jungle of Amazon Basin (selva)

ELEVATION EXTREMES:

Lowest Point: 0 m (Pacific Ocean)

Highest Point: 6,768 m (the mountain Nevado Huascaran)

HEALTH AND SAFETY

Personal Health

Dietary Precautions

Medications & Vaccinations

Safety

PERSONAL HEALTH

Some very important things to remember while on your trip:

1. Drink lots of water to keep from dehydrating, especially if you are in Quito or high altitude. Altitude will cause problems like headaches, tightness of chest, dizziness, and shortness of breath.

2. Apply sunscreen on a regular basis, especially on work sites.

3. Apply clothing in layers as the weather changes rapidly.

4. Use bug repellant.

DIETARY PRECAUTIONS

Water: Drink only bottled or filtered water.

Food: Wash fruits and vegetables using Kil-all, Vitalin, Cloro (1/2 cap full to a sink full of water). If you can peel it, you can eat it (bananas, oranges, apples). Cook meat thoroughly.

Restaurants: Don't eat food bought off the streets. "Menu" specials are always a good economic value, and it is generally safer to order bottled water or soda. If you order juice or drinks with ice, ask if they used purified water.

MEDICATIONS & VACCINATIONS

What shots or medications do we recommend?

Hepatitis A and B

Tetanus/diphtheria (every 10 years, or at least a booster shot)

Yellow Fever

- Not needed in the mountains

- Recommended for both the beach and the jungle

- It must be done 10 days before the trip to be effective

- It is good for 10 years

Malaria pills

- Not present in the mountains nor in Trujillo

- You may want to take Malaria pills. You can buy pills at Hospital Voz Andes, take 2 pills a day, starting 2 days before you leave, through 2 days after you return. If you have Malaria pills prescribed by your doctor, follow their instructions.

- A personal decision can be made on malaria pills, only after discussing it with a doctor

- Chloroquine resistant malaria is present at low elevations

Numavax (over 65 years old)

- Same as in North America

Rabies

- 3 doses

If you have problems with your heart or blood pressure, be sure to get clearance from your doctor. If you are going to Quito, it is 9,500ft above sea level, and that can affect your breathing.

If you have a tendency to altitude sickness, you should discuss the use of Diamox with your doctor.

Changes in the climate, food, and water may cause some digestive upsets. You may want to bring some medication for this, and we recommend Ciprofloxacin, 500mg. If, and when, diarrhea starts you should begin taking Ciprofloxacin (one pill every 12 hours), and notify an Inca Link team leader. Some people recommend taking acidophilus pills two weeks prior to your trip.

SAFETY

The following are general safety tips to decrease the odds for being the target of a robbery or crime:

1. Always be aware of your surroundings.

2. Do not be "the easy target" or the idea of "risk reduction." (90% of all crime can be deterred)

3. Develop a security consciousness.

4. Maze or pepper spray is good to have handy.

5. Walk on the outside of the sidewalk.

6. Do not withdraw large amounts of money alone.

7. Do not go to the same bank at the same time, every time-vary your schedule.

8. Scams:

- "You dropped some money" – especially after coming out of the bank, someone will point out money on the ground and ask you if you have dropped it.

- You hear a sound and someone outside holds up a bolt motioning that your car is falling apart and that you should pull over, DO NOT.

- You are side swiped and the other party demands or motions you to pull over to check damages – DO NOT.

- In both situations, keep windows up and doors locked at all times. If you do stop or are forced to, let them talk through the window and if you have a cell phone call someone.

- In a restaurant, "something on the floor"– or ketchup/mustard on the shirt, this is a distraction, while someone else robs you.

9. Be aware when returning from trips alone. They scout potential victims at the airport especially.

10. Be aware that you are being watched – do not show your money in public, be careful with jewelry, etc.

11. When riding in public transportation, keep your backpack in front of you and be aware of the people around you. Find a spot where you are against the wall or seat and not another person – if possible.

12. Ladies especially, when taking a taxi alone, especially at night, take note of the taxi number and call it in on your cell phone to a friend or fake it.

13. Take a taxi from a Cooperative or call for a taxi.

Learning safety tips does not replace trusting the Lord; we are here because we trust Him. Let's do our best to engage in our God given senses, as we trust Him every day.

GENERAL INFORMATION

CELL PHONES

Each intern will be provided with a cell phone. When calling from cell to cell it is cheaper than calling cell to home. In Ecuador cell phone numbers start with 09, and when dialing a home number from a cell, you must dial 02. Please be wise when using your cell phone, and use it mostly in cases of emergencies. You can buy cell phone cards off the street at most major intersections from the guys dressed in blue and green, or from an CNT or Movistar store. If your cell phone is CLARO, then buy from the red dressed guys on the side of the street.

INTERNET

You should have access to internet fairly often. There is wifi in CasaBlanca and possibly at the Children's Home in Peru. There are also internet cafes all over town. You may use the internet there, and they will charge you for the amount of minutes you are online. If you are in Quito: Train Stops, Cinemark, Nazarene Seminary and Casa Blanca all have wifi. If you are in

Trujillo: Starbucks, Downtown Café, America Sur Church, and Larco all have wifi.

VISAS

Anyone entering into Ecuador or Peru for 3 months or less, do not need to apply for a visa. You will receive a tourist visa upon entry for free. If you are staying in one country for longer than 3 months, you will need to apply for a visa, which is usually around $150 for a year, but do not need to do this until you are in country. You will also enter in as a tourist.

MAIL

The mail system in South America isn't the most reliable. We recommend you having any letters or packages sent to groups coming down.

LOCAL CHURCHES

When not working with teams, we recommend that you get involved in a local church. Ask for suggestions; there are countless Spanish options. The Browns attend the La Luz church in Quito, and there are 3 main Alliance Churches that we are partnering with in Trujillo –Larco, America Sur, and Porvenir. It is prohibited to go to an English speaking church since you can do that back home. We want you to immerse yourself in the culture and language while you are here.

Quito has many forms of transportation. Most of your traveling can be done by walking and buses and trolley's cost 25 cents each time you get on. Taxis are a great way to travel also; however, it can be expensive. The minimum is $1, or $1.50 if you call a radio taxi like Taxi Amigo. We recommend that you do not walk or take buses or trolleys at night, but use a taxi (esp. women).

Trujillo also has many forms of transportation. Some of your traveling can be done by walking, but buses and taxis are always available too. There are different bus routes to the different ministry sites that will cost s/.50 centimos each time you get on. Taxis are a great way to travel also; however, it can be expensive. You will need to negotiate your price before you get into a taxi, which can range from s/.3-8 in the city, or s/.15+ to the airport or beach. We recommend that you do not walk or take buses at night, but use a taxi (esp. women).

The following are taxis that you may use in Trujillo:

Pastor Jose: 998979621 (Expect the unexpected! He once asked if I would mind holding on to the live chickens that he was buying from Don Juan. Ha!)

Willy: 971688167

Freddy: 956294015

www.ingramcontent.com/pod-product-compliance
Lightning Source LLC
Chambersburg PA
CBHW071748270326
41928CB00013B/2845